It Occurred to Me

It Occurred to Me

A Guide to a Happy Self

∞

CAROL SWARBRICK DRIES

Copyright © 2002 by Carol Swarbrick Dries.

Library of Congress Number:		2002095052
ISBN:	Hardcover	1-4010-7732-3
	Softcover	1-4010-7731-5

All rights reserved. No part of this book may be reproduced or transmitted in any form or by any means, electronic or mechanical, including photocopying, recording, or by any information storage and retrieval system, without permission in writing from the copyright owner.

This book was printed in the United States of America.

To order additional copies of this book, contact:

Xlibris Corporation
1-888-795-4274
www.Xlibris.com

Orders@Xlibris.com

Contents

A Happy Self

EGO IN THE SKIN	18
THE ART OF RECEIVING	23
RELATIONSHIPS	31
ONION SKINS	37
AUTUMN LEAVES	40
COLUMBIA TRIUMPHANT	46
CATERPILLAR-COCOON-BUTTERFLY	56

The "G" Word

ONE IN THE ONE	63
THE PRESENCE	65
DOORKNOBS	69
IT OCCURRED TO NONE OF US	72
"I AM PART OF THE GREAT MIND OF GOD"	82
THE LORD'S PRAYER	87

INTO RECOVERY

THE FIRST THREE STEPS 91

THE ROAD TO SANITY 93

MY SIDE OF THE STORY 97

Dedication

For My Husband, Jim;

A Miracle That Occurred To Me!

A Happy Self

Imagine, if you will, the largest mural you have ever seen. Larger. This mural is so large you have to keep stepping away from it to get any perspective at all, and, even then, you cannot see all of it. It's enormous! As you look more closely, you see that it is not an ordinary mural, it is made up of millions of pieces, different shapes and sizes – almost like a jigsaw puzzle – each piece fitting perfectly into the whole – which you still cannot see. As you come even closer to it, you see there is a gold plaque under the mural, a nameplate. It reads: "Your Greatest Good". But all you can really see is the space right in front of you, TODAY, right now. Even the portion to your left, which is your past, can only be seen through your peripheral vision, your memory, and isn't as clear as TODAY is. The space to your right, the future, is, as yet, open, blank.

Now, you notice there are other people here, too, each of them looking at their own mural/mosaics. And all around you, there are puzzle pieces, lying about, hanging from trees (did I mention there are trees here, too? Well, there are!), some of them just falling from the Heavens. Some are sparkling, shining, some are dusty and have been sitting untouched for a long time, some resemble others so closely that you cannot tell one from another, but there is a slight difference. You pick up a piece and examine it, or you grab it and try to fit it into your mural. Some of them do fit, instantly, some of them have to be turned and reversed for them to fit, some of them have to be cleaned off in order to see their true shape and the right place for that piece in your mosaic. Some of them don't fit at all. These pieces aren't yours. They belong in someone else's mural. Just because you were attracted to it, doesn't mean it is right for you. Put those pieces down and try another. If one of your opportunities winds up in someone else's hands, it can't be lost to you. Sooner or later, but certainly eventually, it will not adhere to the other person's mural, and it will come back to you. If it is yours, you will not go without it. Each person's mural must be complete when they pass over, so you need never feel threatened that someone else is getting a piece that was "meant for you". It doesn't work that way. The design is perfect, and we aren't done until the mural is.

When you step away from the mural/mirror now, you can see that the pieces that have made up this work of art are all of the experiences, opportunities and events of your life. All of your choices. What you also see is that if you picked up a piece that doesn't fit, and crammed it, forced it into the picture where it doesn't belong, then, when the right piece shows up, there is no place in your life for it. You've filled that space with something that doesn't fill it BEST. It's hard to see when we are standing so close to it, but it is there, nevertheless.

When I am "puzzled" about the outcome of a project, or nervous about an upcoming situation, I just have to remind myself that I don't see the whole picture. There is One that does, and will make the right piece available to me at the right time. I don't want the wrong piece, because that takes up space without offering me the BEST experience. Not all of my mural/mirror pieces can sparkle. If they did, I would be blinded by the reflection. I want to keep my eyes open to the pieces that fit. I want to keep building on this life-mural with MY BEST choices. Faith that there is One who sees the BIG PICTURE, lets me live, knowing that all I have to do is pick up as many pieces as I can, to see if they fit. The end product is not my business. I can't see the whole thing anyway, so I let go of the results. Then, my hands are free to gather more experiences, opportunities and events.

So often, when misfortune rears its ugly head, people say, "What goes around, comes around". Do we realize that GOOD things come around, too? They do, so long as we have sent them "around". Of course it works both ways. It's part of the LAW. Watch for it. You'll see it. Just for a test, try a smile. What goes around comes around!

Have you ever noticed that when you carry around a lot of resentments, you feel "the weight of the world" on your shoulders? Conversely, have you noticed that when you are feeling grateful for the smallest thing, your load seems lighter? Well, I have, and it occurred to me the other day that they are two sides of the same coin.

When we feel gratitude, our hearts seem to open to all the joy of the world. Nothing is impossible because we are a "Have." Our supply of *whatever* has been met and usually exceeded. Or a sudden gift has come to us. It could be as simple as an unexpected smile. Whatever it is, we are grateful for it. We walk with a lighter step.

On the other hand, if we feel we have been cheated, or misled, or dealt with in a less than respectful manner, we can get resentments. We hold these closely, and are loath to let them go. We "deserve" them and we're going to keep them. After all, that person or situation has kept something we wanted from us. We are "Have-Nots", and we don't like it. It's the "Have-Not attitude" that keeps us from letting go of the bad feeling. It is thinking that we have lost something that is rightfully ours that keeps us from letting go.

Now, we know intellectually that the person or situation is probably totally oblivious to our self-created burden, but that doesn't loosen our grip on it. Do we really think: "Well, if I can't have the thing I want, at least I'll have this bad feeling to hold onto."? I don't think so, but that's how we act.

If we could be grateful for what we do "Have" for what we "Have" received, what we "Have" experienced in joy and love and freedom, perhaps the resentments would dissolve. If we could picture ourselves as "Have-ing" all we need, (because we are given it daily by the Universe), maybe we could let go the bad feelings. Put down the world. Don't pick it back up. Be grateful for the day, the weather ("whether you like it or not") and your life. Find something. Your burden will vanish in a shaft of gratitude. They cannot occupy the same space anymore than light and darkness can. Gratitude and Resentments are two sides of the same coin. Choose which one you will look at.

Thank you!

The other morning, it occurred to me that when a flower is hit by a raindrop, it reacts. Maybe it even stings the petal. I don't know. I'm sure if I were more sensitive to plants, I would hear them shriek with the pain of being pruned. But in order for the plant or the flower to grow to its true and greatest potential, it must suffer the drops of rain, or it will die. It must endure the careful, studied pruning to direct its growth. It is so similar to what I am going through, and perhaps, you, too. Some of the necessities in my life are delivered in such a way that they sting me. On a bad day, I resent it. On a good day, I know it is just a spring rain, and I am reminded that the raindrops and the pruning are actually ensuring my growth.

EGO IN THE SKIN

Well, here's a theory I've been working on: The ego is contained in our skin. Now, I'll tell you why I am proposing this theory.

For the longest time, and at the odd moment, I have had thoughts about what people would say or do if I should pass away at that moment. (Haven't you, too?) Well, then, it occurred to me that it wouldn't matter to me what they said or did, because I would have no EGO invested in their reactions anymore. I would have doffed "this mortal coil". Without my *skin*, I would probably throw back my non-existent head and laugh at what I thought was so important when I did have skin. Do you see what I mean? Once we leave our bodies, we leave our egos behind, too.

To take this idea a step further, think of how much of our ego is wrapped up in our skin, and what our skin wraps up (!). So much of our ego is entwined with how we look, how we are built, what color we are, how firm our skin is, how smooth it is, how tight or saggy it is. We begin to believe that we are our *skin*. How MUCH does our skin have to cover? Do we have too much skin-surface? That is, do we weigh too much, are we too fat? Do we have wrinkled skin because we are too old? How do we appear to others? These are questions of the ego, and it all involves our skin.

Before we are born, before we are wearing this skin, we have no ego. We know all there is to know, and we see the universe without shadows or disfigurements. Our skin casts the shadow and creates the disfigurement. The skin hides our true beings and presents *seeming* imperfections, disfigurements. The skin is what we look at. We tend to not look within – not ourselves and not others. When we stop looking *past* the skin, we accept-as-real cosmetic concerns. We say things like: "I'm going to the gym because I am respecting myself," or "I like myself better when I wear more make-up." Now, I am not saying that these are out-and-out lies, but they are, too often, justifications. If our motivation is our outer appearance rather than our inner health and awareness, then, our egos are in control. The *image* we present has become more important than the *substance* of our beings. Beauty is only skin-deep when it is ego-based and ego-maintained. When we judge ourselves or others by our skins, we are deeply entrenched in the ego.

So, what's a body to do? Well, we might acknowledge our ego-shell, and then reach inside and love our-Selves, our inner Selves. Once we recognize how shallow the ego is, we can dive into the meat, the hearts, of our-Selves. Without this outer layer/ego, other's colors, sizes and shapes will be less threatening. It is scary to think where our egos have taken us. Is it scary enough to "jump out of our skins" (leap out of our egos?) and look beyond the shadows?

Yes. Just this once: DON'T look before you leap!

It occurred to me one day that the reason I am so grateful for my life is that my life is great-full. It is not merely fine-full or okay-full, it is GREAT-full. My life is full of great friends, great family (whether by blood or by bond), great memories, great opportunities, great possibilities. Great music surrounds me when I use the radio or tapes or cd's. Great aromas greet my sense of smell, great vistas are there for me to see, great sensations are awaiting my touch, great spices and seasonings tantalize my taste-buds. I look up at the great sky, into which I can throw all of my great cares and concerns – knowing that they will be dealt with in the greatest of ways by the Greatest of All. When I think of all the great gifts I have been given in these (great) many years, I would be remiss were I NOT grateful. Likewise, my life is wonder-full, respect-full, and just plain filled with "full." I guess that's why I feel so full-filled.

When I was in school, the word "integer" was used in Arithmetic courses. An integer is a whole number, as opposed to a fraction. I have not thought about this word for years, but recently, it occurred to me that "integer" is the root word for "integrity." We are expressing our whole nature when we act with integrity. In our dealings with others and ourselves, if we cheat, steal or lie, we are offering only a portion, a small fraction, of what we are. It's not limited to "honesty" or "kindness." That is part of the whole, but *integrity* suggests that the whole picture is considered, that you are entirely represented, that "the truth, the whole truth, and nothing but the truth" is being offered.

Without integrity, our beings begin to dis-*integrate*. The wholeness is lost.

When any of us gets involved with obsessive, addictive or compulsive behaviors, we begin to believe that we are "less than . . . " . We begin to believe that we are not whole beings. Many experience it as having a hole in their souls. The truth is that there is not a soul-hole there, but a soul-WHOLE. It is our "stinking thinking", our self-judgments, and often our reliance on others' opinions of us that have driven a hole in our self-*image*. It is hard to see it as a hole in our *imag*-ination rather than in our-*selves*, however, when negative habits have us moving in a downward spiral. It is important, nay, essential that we reverse this motion and realize our entirety, and our independence. In the English language, the first person singular pronoun is "I". The Roman numeral for One is also "I". If I can think of myself as "I" in English and Roman numerals, I am a straight, strong pole, (A "Divining Rod"? No, I go too far!) There's a base on the bottom on which I can stand and a large flat receptor on the top, by which to accept Divine Messages. One (1) is a whole number, and I can stand alone.

It is a simple concept. Are you living as a whole number or a fraction?

THE ART OF RECEIVING

"It is better to give than to receive." Well, who doesn't know that? We all hear it, learn it and try to live by it. So much so, I think, that many of us have lost the ability to *receive* with grace. We have forgotten that the Universe works in circular motions. Yes, it is true that in order to receive, one must be willing to give. But, what about the willingness to *receive*? When was the last time a friend or associate offered you a compliment, a helping hand or a non-essential gift? How did you take it? Did you take it? Or did you deflect the compliment, reject the help and suspect the gift?

What a pity.

I remember when I was in my 20's, I did some volunteer work for my church. I would go in every morning and do simple clerical work. (This was a bit difficult for I had a night job at the time, but I was inspired by our minister and wanted to *give*.) Some months later, the minister's wife saw me working at my desk and asked me for my Social Security number. I gave it to her, but asked why she had requested it. She explained that they intended to put me on the payroll. "You have a need to give, and now it is our turn." She said it so simply that there was no room for retort. It was time, also, for me to receive.

I still have trouble with this. I go through questions of worthiness. I ask myself if the giver is sincere in his/her giving. I feel somehow more comfortable in receiving if I can reduce the gift to an emotionally manageable value, if I can "pay" for the receipt by giving back, by reciprocating, by *doing* more! This action diminishes *the gift* that your gift-giver should have received by giving. Do you see how the obligation you have assumed in receipt of the gift decreases the enjoyment of giving?

A gift has NO strings attached. If there are strings, it is a ploy, a bargaining chip or a loan with a very high rate of interest. It is not a gift. So, accept with grace. Sounds easy doesn't it? Well, there are few of us for whom receiving is graceful. Hmmmmm. Grace-ful. How do we receive Grace? Does it not just land on us like soft snowflakes? Is it not bestowed on us simply because we are? Can we not accept a present from a loved one or an acquaintance as an acknowledgement of who we are – or at least who we were to that person on one particular occasion?

Can we recognize the difference between being receptive and acquisitive? This is another area that needs clarification if we are to develop the art of receiving. Grasping, clutching, coveting. These are not words that describe receiving, they are words of acquisition. Big difference. Accepting is graceful, acquiring is get-ful.

Does this confuse you? Probably. Because we have been conditioned to feel that we should not accept acknowledgement, much less thanks, for *being*, just being who we are. It's too easy. It's not enough. We should have to work harder to get something. Yikes! When was the last time *you* had coffee with a Puritan? Why do so many of us still attach ourselves to their Code of Ethics??? Is it conceivable that the gift-giver does know what he/she is doing? Is it imaginable that he/she wants to say something that is more easily said by making or purchasing a tangible present than formulating a phrase? Is it possible that you have positively impacted a life when you were not aware of it, and that by denying the gift, you deny the impact?

Allow the joy of giving. In fact, if it's easier, think of your acceptance of a gift as a gift in itself.

I am performer by profession. Some time ago, I worked with a young, talented and beautiful woman who felt uncomfortable taking her curtain call. She didn't feel she should walk out onstage with the express purpose of being applauded. I suggested to her that the audience wants to say "Thank You", especially to performers who have touched them. Their language is applause. If she were not to take her bow, the audience's efforts to thank her would be thwarted. She would be preventing their opportunity to give. I suggested that she think of her bow as saying, "You're welcome" to the audience. She seemed pleased with that. As result, she gave me a gift. I graciously received it.

You are good. Your good intentions do get rewarded – sometimes by other human beings. Allow them the joy of giving. Provide others with the pleasure you get when you give. Allow it. Take it. As you give, (i.e., gracefully, joyously, freely,) so shall (should) you receive.

When change comes
It is important to remember
That we are not LOSING
We are LIVING

Don't you find WORDS to be absolutely fascinating? I do. The spelling of WORDS, the juxtaposition of the letters in the WORDS. For example, "humiliate" and "humility". The difference in the letters is tiny, but the difference in the meaning is mighty. It would be so tidy if the difference were involving the letter "i". Instead, the difference is in the concept "I". (Didn't you just know I would make this work out?) The only way a person can be "humiliated" is if they are holding onto false pride – ego. It occurred to me one morning, that I do this. I do not *want* false pride, but in my everyday dealings, I find that I work very hard to protect it! Yes, I fear economic decline. I fear the end of romantic relationships, I fear the loss of a job. BUT, I do not really believe there is any chance I will be living on the streets, or alone-for-life, or "never to work again". What I really fear is that I will be found to have made some errors in judgment – that I have been im-perfect in ALL of my dealings. I fear the embarrassment, the "humiliation". Once I realized that, I reverted to "humility", and gave thanks for all that I have, for the lessons I have learned, the joy I have experienced. I can acknowledge the faith that has been built out of all of these experiences. In "humility", I can laugh at myself, lovingly, for expecting perfection from myself at every turn. (I remarked to my husband recently, that with age, I have learned to laugh at myself. He replied that with age, there is so much more to laugh at!) In humility, the letter "i" is maintained. The Self remains, but the ego is lifted out of the situation when we become humble. With the ego removed, there is room for growth in the situation.

Another pair of words that have caught my attention recently is: "complete" and "complement." Now, in our couple-oriented society, many of us have been convinced that the only way to have *completion* is to be paired off. (Well, the very phrase "paired off" suggests to me that one is dispensed with or set aside once one is "paired off." I don't much care for any circumstance which disregards me!) At any rate, the word "complement" means adding to, augmentation. Also, if we look at the other spelling of "compliment" we think of something that "comes with". On a menu, a "complimentary" beverage or dessert comes with the meal – at no cost. One doesn't have to work or pay for the beverage or dessert. It is "complimentary." So, to pursue this line of thinking, one does not have to work for a complement, an augment – a partnership. Both parties must work *on* and *with* a relationship, but if one is working *for* a relationship, the work will likely prove futile. One must first and foremost work for real-izing one's own *comple*tion. Then, the complement will appear. Do you see that when we insert the word "men" (and in this discussion, we're using the generic "men") into the word "complete", the result is "comple*men*te". The result is not more whole, essential or complete. The result is augmentation.

To summarize then, nowhere in the word "complete" is there any lack or need of an-other. No, we are all complete within ourselves. So, society (and we are all partly responsible for the attitudes of our society) has misled us. There is no gap to be filled, no need for another person in order to be complete. The augmentation that occurs with an-other can be wonderful and fulfilling, but shouldn't be confused with completing. That job is done.

RELATIONSHIPS

What do you think of when you hear the word "relationship"? Do you think of romance? Friendship? Honesty and openness? Commitment/responsibility?

Okay, what do *feel* when you hear the word "relationship"? Is it fear? Is it comfort? Peace?

Most of us think in terms of interpersonal relationships: those with our parents, children, spouses and co-workers. Good. How do we relate?

Actually, as defined in the Oxford Dictionary, relationship means "1) fact or state of being related . . . . a connection or association . . . . emotional (esp. sexual) association between two people." So, although most of us think and feel in terms of a personal relationship, *everything* is in relationship in time, space and emotions. When the discussion is broadened to include all people, places and things, there is less expectation and emotion connected to the word. As a result, we can take the blinders off and use our peripherals to their fullest extent.

Think, if you will, about the solar system in which we all reside. The planets all have a *relationship* to the sun. The planets, as well, have satellites, moons or rings related to them. All of these relationships are maintained by an attraction, an actual pull, from the center. So, even though the planets are in their own independent orbits with their own exclusive orbiters, in order to maintain balance and harmony, these *relationships* must remain consistent.

Now, consider that you are the sun in your own solar system. (This is not an exercise in ego-inflation. Each of us is, in fact, the center of our own universe, so try to think of it this way for this discussion.) Each person, place and event in your life is revolving around you. And, each has its own path/orbit, with its own satellites.

What is the attraction for your satellites? What draws your moons into your atmosphere? The purest (and most naïve, I'm afraid) answer to that is "Love". The greatest reasons for a relationship are honesty, caring, openness and communication. (Note, please, the root of communication is "commune": to feel in close touch with another.) To function together harmoniously for the benefit of All. To co-operate. All the planets are independently circling the sun. No one has to sacrifice a moon in order to fit.

Unfortunately, after some experiences in less-than-loving *relationships*, we tend to approach new ones with fear and anxiety. We develop agendas and expectations for one another. We call it "caution". Sophistication takes the place of sensitivity, and cynicism prevents sincerity. We begin to pull in our satellites, for fear of losing them. We hide our stars because we believe they are not brilliant enough. The result is that we become inaccessible and fragmented, thus, our own magnetism is blocked. We are knocked out of our orbits.

Instead of love, *need* becomes the powerful force. Whenever need becomes more prevalent or important than love, the balance is shifted. This can be the case in any of the above-mentioned relationships. For example, there is a powerful dynamic between parents and children of the same sex. There is too often comparison and competitiveness. Parents of the opposite sex often demand an over-abundance of reliance and/or abusive bonding. Between spouses, there can be unhealthy co-dependence, distrust that stems from the unrealistic and unfair expectations. In the employment arena, there is so much fear, distrust and dishonesty that *integrity* becomes nearly impossible, and integrity is essential in order to maintain the harmony and balance of any healthy solar system/relationship.

When we start making changes in ourselves *in order to fit into* a relationship, integrity is lost. These aren't really compromises, though that is how we refer to them. They are sacrifices. We are giving away a part of our beings because we perceive those parts to be objectionable. Instead of being amenable and flexible, we dis-integrate. The result of this process is that we can then offer less to our relationships. Now the orbits are really out of whack! The sun/center has been so maligned, so convoluted, that the planets (your world) are sent into outer space and no one can find YOU.

When embarking on a new relationship, or re-vamping an old one, we have to exercise our own integrity. You know, the root word for integrity is integer: a whole number. Not a part or portion, but the whole pie! It is easy to see how society, parents, spouses/mates and co-workers can chip away at our image of ourselves as total, but in order to function fully in any relationship, we must arrive at the outset as complete beings.

So, it seems to me that the first relationship that must be established is (you guessed it) the one with yourself. Now, I know you have heard this before, and it always seems to be an impossible task. Don't flee. There is some good news. Lots of good news.

First of all, there is no time limit on establishing this relationship, in fact, the process continues as long as you do. Also, you never have to wait for the other person to get off the phone or come back home. YOU are always there. Whenever you have some spare time, the focus of your relationship is right there with you, because it is you.

Here's a starting place for your self-examination: I. Simply the name you call yourself. "I". The Roman Numeral for the number one is "I". You are always whole. You – alone – are enough. In fact, you are plenty, and it's high time you got to know YOU. What is your favorite color? Not the one your father liked best. How do you like your eggs in the morning? Do you like eggs in the morning? What are your preferences? Do an interview on yourself, and recognize all the wonderful experiences you have had, all the events you have survived and the adventures in which you have taken part. They won't all be triumphs, but they can be building blocks – but not if you're not aware of them.

Do some writing. No matter your age or experience, try writing your own memoirs; your recollections. That's it: Re-collect your storehouse of memories.

Resist the temptation to blame others for your life experiences. You are, after all, the common denominator in all of them. You were the one reacting to situations, you are the one who remembers it just that way. (How many times have you and a sibling or close friend revisited the same event only to find that your memories are totally different? Neither is "right" or "wrong", they're just different.) So, recall your own past and get to know yourself. Fall in love, if you will, with yourself. Become aware of all the many cute, lovable traits that you have. Take your time, because you are getting into one of the most important and most enduring relationships of your life. (The other "most important and most enduring relationship" will be with your God, but we'll deal with that in some other essays.)

"I don't know your last name yet,

But I think I want it."

For the longest time, I had "selective deafness". When anyone would say, I was "too tall", I would not hear the rest of the sentence. I am quite tall for a woman, 5'10", without shoes or socks, and I heard that comment a lot. I heard it so often, in fact, that I no longer considered myself "tall", instead. I was "TOO tall." Then, one day, while discussing being "vertically challenged", it occurred to me that I should open my ears (and mind) to the rest of those sentences. What I wasn't hearing were the specifics, and the errors in these comments. I was "too tall" – for their project, or "too tall" for that item of furniture or, oftentimes, "too tall" in someone else's estimation or opinion. I was not "too tall" for me. I was – and am – the perfect height for me. I am the perfect weight for me, today. All the statistics about me are perfect, for today, for me. I am not an error. I am a work-in-progress, and for today, I am at the perfect place for me in that progression. That's ACCEPTANCE, and it's a big relief. I recommend it.

ONION SKINS

For those of us fortunate enough to be alive for a considerable number of years, there is one thing that is guaranteed, one that is quite possible, and one that is simply a gift. They are all processes.

The first is aging. Yes, depending on one's gender and genes, this process starts anywhere from the late twenties to the early forties. But, it's gonna getcha, and once it starts, it continues. There are various ways to slow the process, to mask the process, but it won't be stopped.

The second is maturation. As we know from characters like "Peter Pan", not everyone is affected by maturity, but most of us are. It is the process by which we become responsible for our own decisions and the causes and effects that come to the fore in our lives. This one can take place at any period in our lives. Any. Some people start to grow-up at a very early age. For some of us, this doesn't occur until we are stooped over and slowed down. Most of us start maturing somewhere in the middle. This, too, is a process and doesn't have a stopping point. And, this one is quite possible.

The third, and most exciting, is enlightenment. This is a gift. It is the freedom we are given when we let go of the bondage of self, when we discard what no longer fits our needs and dreams.

It is like the peeling away of onion skins. Our consciousness expands, making the former encasement unsuitable. The old views are too narrow, too confining. The old skin splits and the new one is exposed. The process has started, and the "new one" serves until it, too, becomes too rigid to accept our broader concepts. So, the outer layer is stripped away again. What we see happening is that our inner layers keep expanding to fill and exceed our former boundaries.

Think about your first little apartment or dormitory room. It was great for a while. It was fitting. But, in time, you needed more space. The old, formerly-suitable home had to be replaced by a roomier one. One that could hold your new acquisitions. Readying yourself for that change was probably exciting, but it was also quite a task.

You had to re-view all of the things you brought originally to that new home. What about all that was acquired while you were there? This has to be considered as well. Do you need to take all of it along, does it still serve you? Or should you discard some of it? It is an arduous process, but a necessary one in order for you to *move* on.

This process is not without pain. Compare it to a sunburn, when the skin peels. Depending on the depth of the burn (or the depth of the new awareness), the pain can be excruciating or barely noticeable. Your integrity, your-Self, remains intact, however, throughout these transformations. You have just moved on to larger accommodations. Your Mind expands again and again, and the shedding continues. Epiphanies take the place of ignorance and resistance. Awakenings nurture and grow our awareness, and the old dictates slip away. The safe harbor of dogma opens to an ocean of Spiritual adventure.

Eventually, there is no more skin. Here is just awareness. This is when there is truly no separation. There is a permeable membrane of consciousness that allows each of us to express and experience as our-Selves, but, also to merge and understand. There is only union. We are a whole part of the Whole.

AUTUMN LEAVES

In an Autumn past, I was staring through a window at trees. It was a somewhat windy day and the leaves on the tree just beyond my window were falling. I became fascinated by the dropping of the leaves. It seemed so arbitrary. Which leaves fell was not determined by the color change nor the position on the limb. I continued to stare. I began to wonder how the leaves "decided" to fall. It occurred to me that this was a perfect example of "Letting Go."

The process of letting go could be seen from two perspectives. First, the leaves. How did they know when to fall? When was it the right time for them to let go of the stem or branch to which they had depended? It was effortless. The breeze blew, and a couple or few more fell. Some parted from the tree with one wisp of wind. Others loosened with many passes of air, and some seemed to hang on. Which was I?

Each leaf that fell, drifted peacefully to the earth, to be useful in the growth of another, future life. None broke or were destroyed in the fall. Could I, I wondered, have the faith of a leaf? Could I let go, knowing that I would not break or be destroyed? Could I aid in the growth of a present or future life by simply letting go of the tree on which I had depended?

I find a security in attachments. I tend to hang onto situations, relationships and ideas of my past because of this perceived security. Long after the condition, person or thing has served its purpose in my life, I know that I hold on. So, when I watched this process of Autumn, I had to ask myself how my intelligence compared with that of the leaves. I was not denigrating my intelligence really, just my "intellect." I realized how helpful I could be to myself by looking at the myriad situations and concepts I depend on. If the Universal Source could be trusted to deliver all of these falling leaves safely to another place of life, then why should It not be trusted with my Life? Many of the ideas I had depended upon, had hung onto, have become outmoded and useless. If I can release myself from these ideas, I will allow myself to pass to a better place for my development. At the same time, I will be of greater service to others. On the other hand, if I continue to cling to dead branches, I, too, will die.

Then, I looked at the same process, this time from the perspective of the tree. How many leaves had I sprouted from my branches? If I consider my experiences as branches, and the leaves as concepts and judgments, I could ponder the appropriateness of any continued attachment. Many of my leaves have changed, wilted and dried, but I continue to hang onto them, because of the initial reason for acquisition. "It was good once, so it must be good still." Rather, I should ask myself, "It was good once. Is it still good?" Is it vital and serving me today? I need to pay attention to all the emotional and intellectual concepts I have held, and see if they are still valid. Here, too, I tend to hang onto that which

I have acquired because it makes me feel secure and/or more successful. In actual fact, it makes me feel more comfortable because it is familiar. That's not good enough. What is true for me *now?* That's the active, alive question. That takes some time, effort and work, but if it is not for my growth today, it is time to move on. Time to let go. Make room on those branches for more and newer leaves. New growth.

This is, of course, a lifelong process. Nature, in all of Its wisdom and timelines, gives us a perfect reminder. Each Fall, I can look to the trees and the leaves for inspiration to re-evaluate. Its similar to Spring-cleaning. Each Fall, let the old – fall! Let go, and let's go!

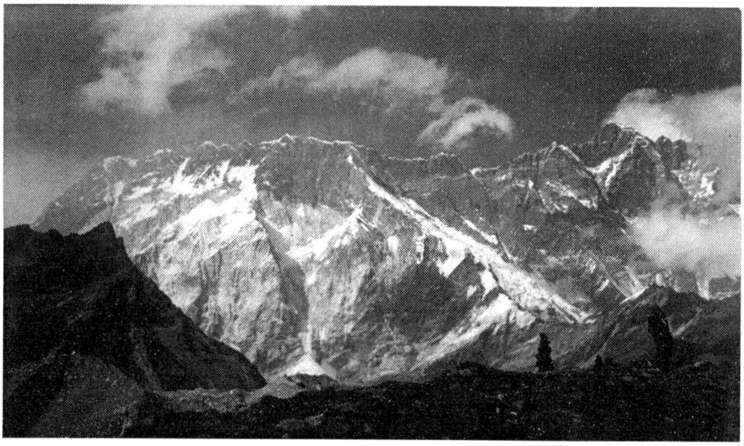

One day, while lying out in the sun, I watched the clouds over my head. I was in an area where they were experiencing a semi-drought, and the clouds I watched were gray. Watching clouds is a fascinating exercise, because they all appear to be at the same level – all together, but in watching their movement and changes, one realizes that they are in quite different places, on different levels – each moving at a different and distinct rate. The gray clouds looked threatening, ominous – as if rain was imminent. It did not rain that day, and the clouds continued to move and change, some of them disappearing from my sight.

It occurred to me, on that afternoon, that just because I had expected those clouds to make rain, and just because rain would have relieved the semi-drought condition, the fact that they didn't open up and spill water onto the land did not make the clouds failures. The clouds were just clouds – being exactly what they were meant (or "supposed") to be. They moved on, as they had been moving since they became clouds, and joined with other clouds, or dissipated, or a myriad of other changes they may have made. But MY expectations not being realized did not make them failures.

How like each of us! The non-realization of expectations from our parents, teachers, friends, lovers – or even from ourselves – does not make us failures. It makes the expectations unrealized. That's all. We move on, joining with other beings, and changing in a myriad of ways, as we have since we became these beings – unless we paralyze ourselves with feelings of failure. I choose to keep moving, at my own level and my own distinct rate. It's exactly what I am meant (and "supposed") to do!

COLUMBIA TRIUMPHANT

Now, it's just you and I here, and I'm not looking, so we both can be perfectly honest. Are you single? Whether or not you have ever been married, or if you are married now, do you feel "single" now? Is it conceivable that if you are or do, you are embarrassed by this status? The reason I ask is that, recently, I realized that more than being *alone*, I was embarrassed by my "single-hood". In my personal scenario, I have been married, and up until rather recently, I was in a devoted and satisfying relationship. In transitioning out of the romantic relationship, I went through the trauma of severing ties, the trying to forget that we went "there" together, that he bought me flowers for "that", etc. Now, many months after the break-up, I realized that there was no void in my life, no vacuum. I am a very successful, active, healthy woman. So, what was I losing sleep over? It occurred to me that I was embarrassed that I was *single* – again! I had this weird concept that God was disappointed in my marital status, that I had let Him down by being un-spoused. Is it possible that you have held the same mis-conception about yourself? It wouldn't be surprising. I think, for women, especially. We are living in a society that shouts about independent and self-sufficient women, but that still broadcasts versions of "Cinderella" and "Sleeping Beauty" to us as little girls before we even know what "single" is! (Yes, this same society is recognizing the male and female parts of each of us, so the feeling is, perhaps, more universal than I perceive it to be.)

So, there I was, confronted with this picture: My Higher Power weeping with disappointment that I could neither hold onto a mate, nor choose the "Right One". Looking at this picture proved very illuminating. In the photo album-of-my-mind, a "whole woman" was married with children. Then the spots making up this photo started to move around and show the holes in the picture. The corners became frayed and my picture needed re-framing!

Once seeing the picture this way, it was easy to see the flaws. We don't all have the same path, the same photo-finish! For many people, their fulfillment comes when they are mated, some when they are parenting. But it comes DURING the partnership – NOT because of it. They grow WHILE parenting, not just BY it. For others, their progress while alone can be the ideal path. Then, with progress, comes change.

While thinking about the *advantages* to being single, I thought about the speed with which decisions are made. There is not such a need for compromise, or satisfying the needs of more than one. "One" can travel at one's own pace without feeling guilty or smug. Lots of things are accomplished when one is "one." Even long-married folks find this to be true, and are often glad to have their spouses out-of-town for periods of time so that they can catch up on real-izing some of their individual dreams.

Then, I thought of the true *beauty* of being single. Is there anything quite so magnificent, meaningful, poignant or elegant as a single rose? There is no need for more. Yes, some roses are more beautiful in a dozen or more, but some seem to be "just meant" to be alone in a crystal bud vase. If you are single, think of yourself as a single rose, not lacking because you are without the other eleven, but standing quite properly, and acceptably, by yourself. Behold your unique beauty, not dimmed or compromised by an-other. Given the space available to a single [rose], you are allowed to bloom fully, to blossom at your own rate, un-cramped by another's perceptions, needs or predilections.

These thoughts were simmering in my mind when I took a trip to New York City. I traveled on the same days as my best friend, but we neither stayed together, nor took part in all of the same events. I had lots of time alone. I was walking by Columbus Circle one morning, mulling over the "half-empty cup of my relationship-status", when I saw a statue atop a monument at the southwest corner of Central Park. There loomed a majestic goddess-warrior driving three magnificent horses. The sight took my breath away. She wasn't riding in a chariot with her spouse. She NEEDED no mate to rein in the steeds. She was alone and powerful and proud. I knew she was going to be my mentor in my quest for "Single Serenity." I had to learn her name. The New York Historical Society gave me it. She is called "Columbia Triumphant." Indeed!

I Accept, Experience and Express All the Love that is Present in my Life Today.

Post September 11th: Safe Haven

There is so much we don't know about what happened on September 11th. We don't know how many were directly responsible. We don't know what kind of rage and misinformation (and misconceptions) must have been utilized to convince human beings to attempt such dreadful attacks on themselves and other humans. We don't know what went on in the minds of those who died. We don't even know for certain how many died.

What we do know is that we are still alive and have before us many tasks. We also have many opportunities. One of the major opportunities this devastating event brings to all of us is to reevaluate our concept of "Safe". How can we be safe? What does it mean to be safe? These questions had very different answers *then* than they do *now*.

It is no longer enough to have a big bank account or stock portfolio to be safe. Going to the gym, lifting weights, running the track, doing the Nautilus, none of this makes us safe. Winning an award or prize doesn't afford us "safe".

"Safe" has nothing to do with externals. We are learning that this is true. So, is it now impossible to be safe?

No. It is an inside job.

We have relied on "the outside" to provide the appearance of safety for so long that this is going to take a lot of re-thinking. It is also going to mean we must plumb a depth many of us have not admitted to or visited for some time. This uncovering, discovering and recovering is essential if we are going to devise a broader, newer, more real "safe haven." And this process can be absolutely halted by the great barrier: FEAR.

We get into "Fear" whenever we feel un-*safe*. Denial. Anger. Hatred. Arrogance. All of these are expressions of fear. We immediately retaliate against ourselves, or we lash out to falsely bolster our own confidence. The Buddha said "All that we are is the result of what we think . . . . Hatred can never put an end to hatred; hate is conquered only by love." This applies to our thinking, our persons, and our governments.

The retaliation within ourselves is often so fierce that we don't even know it is going on. Because our bolstering is false, it can't do a good enough job, and must continually be intensified. We get tougher, less tolerant. It feels like the anxiety is outwardly caused and exacerbated. It's not. We are building up arms and firing against our own good nature because we feel unsafe.

So long as I had the outer trappings: a comfortable home, friends, an income, etc, I could deny that there were any life-threatening problems in the world. "Not to me."

"They aren't in my backyard." Avoidance and denial are very close cousins, and I could choose to avoid any news items that could stir up insecurity in me. Easy. I'll get busy, (a great way to deny!)

Flashing anger could silence my adversaries (at least temporarily, until I could get out of earshot.) Sometimes my rage looked like passion or conviction. That'll slow down anyone with an alternative thought, argument or outlook.

It has always seemed to me that all hatred stems from fear. Why else would anyone have such a strong reaction to anything? I'm not talking here about the kind of repulsion and sadness engendered by heinous and destructive activities. I am talking about a person's preferences, skin color or beliefs. I am talking about choices of life – or living-style. I am talking about voicing opinions. Hatred of these things begins in fear.

I hung onto my arrogance and self-righteousness for a while. I still fight the impulse to "go there". I am in fear that if my ideas or opinions are wrong, that I will be crushed under the judgment of others. This is simply not a possibility, but it feels that way. So, I defend my ideas by being arrogant! The truth is that other people who would have this "crushing judgment" are too busy figuring out what their ideas and opinions are to judge mine, UNLESS, they are in fear also. At that point, they might get angry, avoid me or hate me. I can't control them, so I have to let that go.

This letting go of control, though, leaves me adrift, if the only place of solace and serenity is outside of myself. Now is the time to go within – with all my might and all my energy. That is the safe place that never leaves me. (Ah! Unless I leave me. That is to say that if I have relied so heavily on avoidance and denial to the point of using chemicals [i.e. drugs and/or alcohol] then I abandon/leave myself. This is not a good time to do that.) This is a time to *find* one's Self, the "still, small voice," your own inner sanctum.

Start by recognizing all your assets, all your good traits, habits and gifts. Whenever you are tempted to degrade or disown your-Self, identify one of the gifts you give to your world uniquely. You must have many. We all do. Put your attention there instead of on the negative. As the old song says: "Accentuate the Positive."

Offer your Goodness to your life. It strengthens it and you. It overpowers the fear. You can find great peace within yourself and your faith.

Whatever happens, YOU are there with yourself. Or to turn that around, your-Self is there with you. What is there to fear??? Nothing can befall you that you (along with your-Self) cannot withstand.

To that end, I absolutely believe that every one of the people who died in the terrorist attacks on September 11, 2001, had decided, on a super-conscious level, that they would give their lives to these events. There were so many stories of the "coincidences" of people who were or were not in the buildings at that hour or on those flights on that day. I don't mean to say that they were at all conscious or that they made even subconscious decisions to leave their loved ones, or to be set up as martyrs, but they were willing to be instruments of delivering these opportunities to all of us. We needed a wake-up call and they offered us, collectively, a very dramatic one.

It must not be a "Total Loss" however. Nothing ever should be. There must be something, many things, to be gained from these horrific events. We didn't learn them before. We didn't learn them in the World Trade Center attack in 1993. We didn't learn them with the terrorist attacks at the Olympics back in 1972. We have yet to learn them. We have now.

What a shame it would be, and what a waste, if we do not. If those lost lives did not provide us with motivation to come to a new understanding of what is important, good and safe! Let the heroic acts, the uniting gestures and expressions of people around the world be the inspiration. Look for the good, first in yourself, then in the world around you. You are safe there. Right there. Wherever you are.

Recently, in conversation with a very dear and wise friend, I commented that life is cyclical. She said that it was cyclical only if we think it will be. After thinking about this for quite a while, I realized that it is NOT cyclical at all. If it were cyclical, it would come back to the exact same place as it had been. As WE had been. And we are never at the EXACT same place where we have been before. Life experience has moved us. It is, however, spiral, and we determine the direction and duration of that spiral by our thinking and our footwork. Certainly events will lead us toward (not BACK to) familiar feelings and/or thoughts, but we are maturing, learning and growing through all of this process, in preparation for new responses to those similar situations. We don't have to react in the same way. Each event, each day, offers us new tools to improve our coping skills, to adjust our attitudes. Every moment offers us the chance to make a new beginning, to change or continue in the direction of the spiral we have created.

CATERPILLAR- COCOON- BUTTERFLY

What is it about the metamorphosis of a caterpillar into a butterfly that I find so touching, so moving? Do you, too? I find myself in absolute awe at the thought that a clumsy caterpillar could wind its way into a beautiful, graceful butterfly.

I think what I find most remarkable is the unshakable faith – of each and every caterpillar. It's uncanny.

Think of it. Just inching along, day after day, a caterpillar is instinctually moved, guided by some unseen Hand, to find a shady spot, a branch, an eave, a place to rest. Leaving the familiar green leaves and sunshine, this furry creature heads to a spot that seems safe for some sort of transformation. Does he know what is going to transpire? Is there any inkling of beauty beyond the dark? Has a parent – or pal-caterpillar relayed to him some sort of message of his destiny? Or does the caterpillar simply follow his instinct?

I put myself in a similar situation. Everything around me can be familiar. Not great, but not unacceptable. I move through my days pretty much as I have for quite a while, and a new thought occurs to me, a new path to follow. Do I have the courage to change EVERYTHING? Do I have the faith to turn my back on what seems to be "fine?" Do I have the conviction for myself to follow my instinct and work for transformation?

Back to the caterpillar. Having arrived at this safe place, he plants himself, hangs himself actually. He begins to spin a delicate shroud about himself and . . . what? Does he reflect? Does he hibernate? Does he relax and let go? As far as I know, there is no certainty about what happens in the cocoon to produce the winged beauty, but I'm sure the caterpillar has little to do with the process. Only willingness.

What would I do in such a place? Could I let go and simply believe that my best was about to occur? Could I accept the natural enfoldment of my inner splendor? Would I be content to wait? Could I be willing to accept the changes needed for my own "best"?

It has been proven that any interference in the process damages it. In whatever stage of the transformation "assistance" is offered, it can halt the progress and actually kill the caterpillar-cocoon-butterfly. Patience and faith are required. But the payoff is breathtaking.

Have you seen a butterfly emerging from its cocoon? What unbelievable beauty and fragility. Patience, again, is exercised as she allows her wings to dry enough to support her new body and frame. Wait. Wait. Believe. Soon.

Now, the breeze that was drying her, lifts her and the wings beat ever-so-gently. The butterfly, this new creature, is aloft. She flies to colorful flowers, grasses and leaves. She is no longer limited to crawling along the ground. Her sights and her vision are far more encompassing, expanded.

Where do I find my "hanging place?" Am I willing to put myself in the dark, believing that my magnificence requires this and nothing more? What are my wings going to look like, and where will they take me? What will I see and experience?

What a wonder. What an example. I am in awe.

The "G" Word

Why would God use me as an Example of how He can Fail?

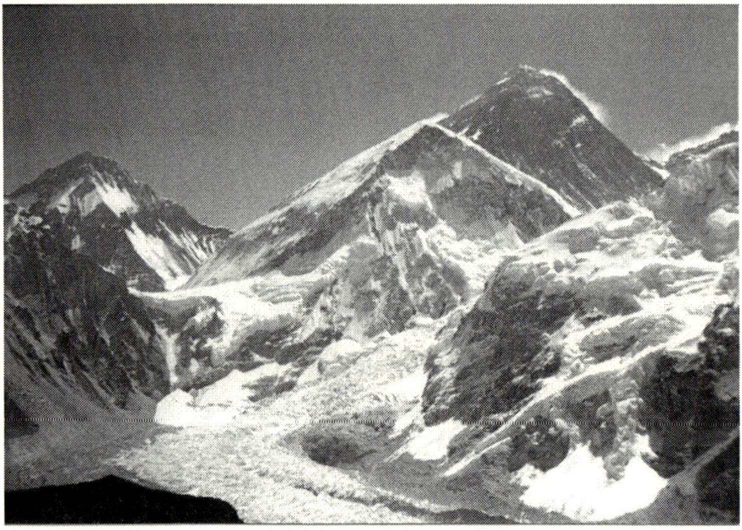

ONE IN THE ONE

For a very long while, I have been trying to reconcile my concept of the Universal Spirit with my own personal God. I have had a very satisfactory awareness of my God, and a fair understanding of the Universal Power, but I pushed aside those thoughts which plagued me about the seeming dichotomy.

What I mean is, when I have a personal, individual dream or concern, how can I expect this Universal Spirit, in charge of ALL THINGS, to hear my prayers? I hear the still small voice, but how can It? Each time I prayed for something, whether for myself or for a dear one, was I being selfish? Was I being egotistical? Why should my concerns or wishes be worthy of Its Attention?

This really bothered me, until the other day, when a new concept began to erupt inside of me. We each do have a God-part. This "part" is very personal, very individual, and quite unique. It is not, however, separate. It is part of the Whole. I call that personal part my Soul. That's it! If my Soul is not made of God, then what is it? That is my eternal, pure part. That is the Light which cannot be diminished or burned out. That is my Life. When I think of my Soul, I know I am one with the Spirit, the Universal Force, with God.

My Soul is entirely involved in my growth, my quest for freedom and awareness. That is the only goal of my Soul, (its sole-goal?): for me to accept and real-ize my Oneness with the All-ness. What a relief. I'm not selfish. I am evolving as Me. I am expressing the Wholeness in my individual way. I am unique without being alone. I am a one-of-a-kind Creation, with my own particular Soul. A part, not apart. One in the One.

Whew!

THE PRESENCE

Like so many of us, I have spent a lot of time and great dedication to real-izing the Presence of God. I have used prayer, readings, trance channeling, meditation and the spoken word to help me to understand the vastness and constancy of The Presence. I don't know if my human mind can grasp the scope of The Law of Good or the Principles of Infinity. I haven't been able to so far.

It occurred to me the other day in Centering Contemplation, though, that my best comparison would be to the Law of Gravity. I can deal with that. I can see it evidenced all around me in my daily life. As long as I keep my thinking to what I know, (that is what happens on this planet,) I can comprehend the vastness, the ever-presence, the constancy of the Law of Gravity. That's how it is with The Presence.

What became apparent to me is that God, as I choose to call this Power, is not something to be attained. The *awareness* of it is to be attained. It is not to be flattered or cajoled or persuaded. It is to be cooperated with and accepted. God *is*. That's it. God doesn't change because of our prayers, we do. The peace we feel when we go into The Silence is not because God has entered, but that we have increased our awareness of The Presence that is there anyway.

You see, God is everywhere present. Constantly. *We* are not ever-aware! That's the inconstancy. "We" not "God." Everywhere. All the time. Just like the Law of Gravity, no one of us or group of us can alter the power of gravity as we know it on earth. It just is. (Some of you may be thinking "What about those chambers where one can experience weightlessness?" Well, they are temporary and fallible and the argument doesn't aid us in understanding The Law, so drop it!) We learn at an early age that the Law of Gravity is present, "where we live, move and have our being." Why do we not concurrently learn that it is thus with the Law of Good?

So, when we go into the Silence, we do not have to reach out for The Presence, neither do we have to reach IN to the Presence. It is there. We have to direct our focus, open our acceptance to the Presence that is there and always has been and always will be. It's an energy, but it isn't working more at one time than any other. It just is. It's kind of like the difference between a human be-ing and a human do-ing. When we meditate, we are advised to *be* rather than *do*. The Presence is Be-ing, and Be-ing and Be-ing.

If you have any doubts about the Law being right where you are, think about this: If you are over 35 years old – you KNOW that the Law of Gravity is within and around your body. For this illustration, don't judge it, don't deny it, just acknowledge it. So, if the Law of Gravity is within and around you, so is The Law of Good, or "God". Yes. You. Always.

Now, when we fall, drop something or do something otherwise physically clumsy, we have accidents. We are inescapably responsible for and suffer from our own unawareness and/or lack of cooperation with the Law of Gravity. Likewise, when we do not cooperate with or have a lesser awareness of the Law of God, our spiritual, emotional or physical beings have "accidents". When bad things happen to good people, do we really believe that this is the Will of God? Could we instead be misunderstanding the situation? Are we in a state of diminished awareness? Are we misinterpreting the evidence by our limited scope? Remember, The Law is constant. It isn't productive or encouraging – or even accurate – to say that God is trying to teach us a lesson by our injuries. *We* have not been in the flow of The Law. That's all. It is also not productive or suggested that we beat ourselves up about our "accidents". They are, for the most part, not grievous crimes against man or nature, they are just short of the mark. We have been caught with our Spiritual pants down, focusing on other than the Law. We suffer the consequences, but not from a punishing or arbitrary Tyrant. We face the consequences of our own actions. Many times, the consequences can be less trying and painful if we immediately get back into cooperation and increase our awareness of the Law.

In some situations, we find that our egos have gone to a place where we think we have "The Power." We are bound to have accidents. At times like these, we would benefit most to acknowledge the true Presence and Power, forgive ourselves and turn ourselves around.

It is so freeing to realize that The Law is not capricious, partial or temporary. It works for me the same way it does for a person on the other side of the planet, someone speaking a different language, calling the Power a different name. It's the same.

Find the freedom. Give yourself a break. Stop trying to appease a power that can be altered by praise or chastising; that can be tempted by manipulation and calculations. Relax in the Law of God. It works for everyone. It has to. It's The Law!

"Thy Will, not mine, be done." It is such a simple statement, but a difficult directive. We are taught from the get-go that Efforts get Results. How can we relinquish our will, when that is what motivates us? Who, or What, can be the model to follow in surrendering?

God is the answer. Yes, another simple phrase, but in this case, "God" is the answer to the question posed. The very fact that we have free will is the proof.

When this whole world was made manifest, when the universe became real-ized, God gave us free will. Do you see? He surrendered His Will to us. He gave us eyes to see the options we deal with every day. He gave us access to His Will, and the opportunity to choose His Will. Or not. It wasn't a dictate. It isn't a commandment. It is a choice.

So, when we wonder where to go for an example of "letting go", let us consider the Divine Effort that gave us free will. Now, that's surrender, in its greatest, most magnificent form. Can we make an effort to choose God's Will? It's a choice. We can try.

DOORKNOBS

Do you remember the first time you met "that certain someone"? The first time you received a nod of acceptance in your chosen career, or when you felt truly "at home" in a new church or fellowship? It's like falling in love. You seem to be buoyed up in a bubble of comfort and appreciation. Everything is brighter, and the glow is coming from within you. There is freedom and joy all around you in this place. You are safe here.

The trouble comes when you simply *remember* that feeling. When it isn't re-newed. The memory of the feeling isn't the feeling itself, and your comfort zone becomes hard and firm with the passage of time. What once was a clear view of the world, becomes a glass wall, then a small window, then a window with bars on it and you are hanging on to see the slightest piece of sky.

Now don't be too hard on yourself. It's easy to stay in the past. After all, it can be romanced! You can't romance the present. So, you re-run the words of the past, the perceptions of yesterday, the promises that were. What was once a fluid freedom, becomes a prison cell of the past. Do you find yourself there in any situation in your life? If you feel like you are standing at this tiny window, look just to the side of it and see the calendar. If it doesn't have TODAY written on it, turn around and leave.

You can. Just turn around, the door is open. Funny, though, it slams shut as soon as you are out. Now you are in what I call "The Hallway of Opportunity". You've heard the saying, "God never shuts a door, but He opens another one." Well those are the "another" doors that line this hallway. You have now moved out of the past, and are offered all sorts of options.

Here's the one prerequisite to opening those doors: you have to let go of the doorknob of the cell you just left. That isn't as simple as it sounds. You had a lot of fun in there, a lot of satisfaction and a lot of reinforcement. So, you aren't sure (yet!) that you really want to let go of the doorknob. Trouble is, you can't reach the next doorway while still holding on.

TRUST. That's the key. ("Key", "Cell", "Doorknob"; this metaphor is going too far!) You have to trust. Ask yourself, "Has My Higher Power ever dropped me when I have trusted It?" "When I have truly listened to the Still Small Voice Within, has it ever lied to me?" "Is God's Will for me to stay in this hallway forever, never knowing what lies beyond those other doors?" The answer to all of these questions is doubtless: "No!" Does that make the letting go easy? Again, the answer is "No." But it can be done, and you can do it.

In my experience, when I envision myself holding onto that doorknob, frightened in the dimly lit hallway, I take a deep psychic breath, and let go. The end of the hallway bursts into light and all the doorways are open to me. It's exhilarating. My arms are outstretched, making my heart available. My hands are open and ready to grasp the "new and improved" door. I have to trust. The Power I call God would not tease me or drop me. I am supported. Just as "God never shuts a door, but He opens another one." My God offers me more than I can hold. I must keep my hands – and my heart – open and receptive. That way they are never empty.

IT OCCURRED TO NONE OF US

It occurs to me that it did NOT occur to me, i.e. that it did NOT just happen – not to any of us, rather, that we planned the circumstances of our lives. Yes, all of them. Also, I agree with the Buddhist philosophy of reincarnation. It just makes no sense to me that my Spirit would be limited to the experiences of a white woman born in the 20th Century in America.

Here's what I think happens:

When we are between physical incarnations, when we have no ego to confuse us and we can see the Big Picture of our lives, we know what we need. It is as if we are looking at a class schedule for LIFE, and we can tell which classes we need in order to round out our education. So, we choose the courses we can handle – and that we need – in order to progress. (Interesting the use of the word "course" as in "class" and as in "path".)

Say, for example, that in all of your past lives, you have missed the experience of being born into poverty, thus being prevented from having the opportunity to prevail over financial hardship. Just for example. Then, in between these "lives", you could choose to be born to parents who are financially disadvantaged. Then, in human form, you would be giving yourself the chance to work through this dilemma. Do you see how this explains once again how there are no accidents? How we are not victims, but the ones who determine our challenges? It is not a punishment for being too rich in another lifetime, it is the gift of another experience! In the "Other Realm", we have the opportunity and the obligation to CHOOSE what our lives will offer us.

In my case, I am quite sure that I selected my family: with the probability of a life where I would lose my father when I was 3, where my younger brother had the CHOICE to leave his body, and us, at the age of 25, where my mother became a stronger, more open-minded woman with each apparent tragedy in her life. And on and on. Of course each individual involved has free choice at every turn, but the likelihood was that if I chose this family at that particular time, my life's script would be outlined in the way that it was. No accidents, and certainly no mistakes!

Looking at my life from this perspective allows me to be grateful for my circumstances, rather than bemoaning them. It gives me the chance to look at the situation in which I find myself at any given moment, and look for the lesson in it for me. It could be the most beautiful relationship I've ever known, or it could be the most devastating loss I've ever felt. At either end of the spectrum, I know there are lessons – which I GAVE TO MYSELF – in order to move forward on my path.

It has been suggested, for example, that before this incarnation, I realized that I needed to know that I could thrive without a man. So, I decided to join my birth family and I lost what I considered to be the two most important men in my life by the time I was 22 years old. Now, I certainly didn't see this as a gift. Nor did I immediately "thrive", but I survived. For a while, that was all I did. Then, I grew, and then, I began to thrive. And now, I can thoroughly enjoy a relationship with a man – and know that I don't NEED that for completion, wholeness, happiness or success. I am not sure that that is the lesson I chose, but it seems very likely that it is one of them!

Here's your assignment (if you choose to accept it): Take a look at your life, where you came from, where you are going and the paths you have traveled thus far. What were the lessons you chose? How are you doing with them? Are you committing yourself simply to a Pass/Fail mark, or are you really striving for an A+? What could you do to get "Extra Credit"? It's like a "Take-Home Quiz". Good luck. You wrote it yourself!

Sometimes – more often than I'd like – I get impatient. Things just don't move as fast as I want them to. When I'm expecting an important (to me – NOW!) phone call, I pick up the receiver to make sure my phone is still working. When arrangements are not assured, I feel that I have to wind God's Clock for Him. "What could be taking Him so long to confirm my plans???" I become afraid that I am going to miss the dead-line. I become so frantic, that I cease to think, I just react. "Doesn't God know this has to be done by such-and-such?"

Fortunately, I start my days with journaling, and when I see these non-thinking thoughts appear in my writing, I know I am 'way off-course. I am working on my own fallible clock, not on Divine Order. God will ALWAYS throw me a "Life-Line" long before the "Dead-Line." I won't be forgotten, and the blessings in my plans will not go un-given. I just have to trust, unclench my fists and open my hands to receive the gifts. They always arrive On TIME.

There is an image that was given to me many years ago about "Living in The Presence of God". It is as a loaf of bread in the ocean. This image helps me to understand the Presence inside and outside of me.

You see, we can envision Universal Power – or God, as I choose to call It – as the largeness, the vastness of an ocean. We are like loaves of bread in this ocean, this sea of God. God is all around us – and – as our consciousness permits, in us. Water has long been considered life-giving. Think of becoming totally submerged in this Water. Floating, but within the body of Water, not just floating on the surface. Next allow yourself to envision this Water filling you, that you are saturated with this Presence.

Our ego is like the crust of the loaf. If we CHOOSE to remove ourselves from The Presence, very little can seep in. If we feel that the waves of God have tossed us up on a rock, or have battered us against the shores, we may harden our crusts in defensiveness. We may think we are "doing the best we can" in these situations. In actuality, we are becoming all dried out and isolated in our shell/crust. The "best" thing for us to do when we find ourselves alone on the shore of Life is to dive back in. Trust that Our Higher Power has created us to be buoyed up. As we allow the waters to pour over and all around us, we find that they are flowing through us as well. There is a cleansing, a rushing through our beings, an elimination of unneeded ideas. Negative concepts are washed away with the tide. Naturally, and without resistance, we are clean.

The more we can imagine (image-in) ourselves as the loaves, the less we fight the changing tides, the whirlpools that Life presents to us. We relax and Let God. We find that we are "Living in The Presence."

It was the end of the day, and I was tired. I knew before I went to sleep, even before I got into bed, I would get on my knees to thank God for all the blessings of the day, individually, as best I could recall them. But, I was tired, and didn't want to take time out to do that. Then, I thought, "Will that hurt God's feelings?" (I actually thought that!) It woke me up. Then, it occurred to me that my prayers are not to make God feel better. God does not need my encouragement, or my cajoling. God is not swayed by my pleadings or by my lack of attention. God is not arbitrary. (Thank God!) God is as constant as . . . . well, as constant as LAW. For example, take the LAW of gravity. It doesn't change mid-fall, because a leaf screams "Stop!" (Somehow, I have confidence in the intelligence of plants, that there has never been a leaf to scream "Stop!" mid-fall, but you get the point.) No, the LAW of gravity is constant. Such is God. So, why do I kneel and pray at the end of the day, if not to please God? To remind ME of all the blessings of my day. To allow MYSELF the joys, once again, that played themselves out for me, to reopen the gifts the day has presented to me. It doesn't affect God one way or the other, but it does affect me. I rarely miss the opportunity to relive those moments in my day. Why wouldn't I offer myself that present as often as possible? And in the morning, when I meditate, it is not to get God aligned with ME, it is to get my thinking, my believing, my living in line with The Best. I can wake up with lots of mis-information and misgivings. These go with me into my day, unless I take time – for me – to open my mind to the truth, the goodness, the wholeness that is real. I take time to shed the false, the limiting, the "bondage of self." It's just for ME, because it makes ME feel free, accessible, available to all the opportunities that will present themselves to help me on this path of progress (remember: I am a work-in-progress). So, if it means I get up 30 minutes earlier, I'm worth it – everyday! Even when I think I'm not. I'm not the Decide-er on this one, just the Agree-er!

"Grace" is such a wondrous thing. It isn't earned or deserved, it is freely given. It is like standing under a waterfall, no matter who we are, what we look like, or what we have done, the water will pour over us. What keeps us from standing under the waterfall? Most of the limits we feel in our lives are self-imposed. Do we ever stop to consider that there is enough sunshine for us each to get a tan? We just need to take the time to soak up those rays! So it is with the blessings around us. There are enough blessings and gifts for us all to feel, and truly BE blessed. All we need to do is open our hearts and our lives to them, and we receive. When we open our eyes to this actuality, we see it. It is there. Look!

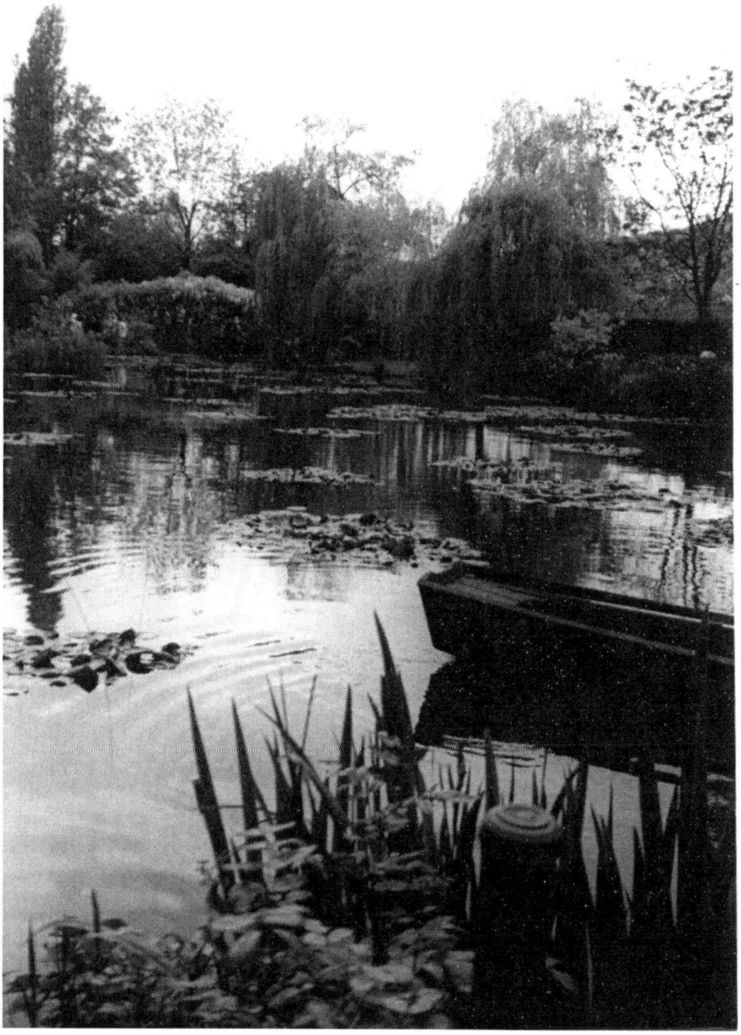

"I AM PART OF THE GREAT MIND OF GOD"

There is a lovely little song we sing in church that begins with that line of lyric. It has become my mantra and leads me easily into a meditative frame of Mind. Join me, if you will, on a journey to your own "Within."

I am a very visual person, so I begin to "envision" a sphere. Now, my Higher Power, whom I choose to call "God", is infinite, but our minds cannot conceive of a Presence without bounds. So, I use this sphere to represent God. This sphere is flexible and fluid, and each of us has a part in it. That's what the song says. "I am *part* of the Great Mind of God." So, imagine a space that is just for you, on the surface of the sphere. There is space enough for *all* of you, the wholeness of you. You can make this space any size or shape you wish. It is *yours*. (Since I am an actress, I envision a space in the shape of a star.)

Once you have established your "part", you can imagine

lifting it out, away from this surface. That way, you can see the gap that your absence creates. You get a sense of how essential your presence is to the Whole. Just as you are not a fraction, you are also not disposable. Without you, the Whole is not complete! You belong there/here. So, put yourself back in the sphere, and notice how your edges meet those of the other parts around you. Your sides *merge* with the surface. You and the surface, you and Spirit, are One.

So many times in work and/or romantic relationships, we start to chip away at our abilities, our gifts. In an effort to "get along", to "not make waves", we minimize our-Selves. We treat our unique gifts as if we purchased them at a store. We try to turn them in, oftentimes not even asking for an exchange, just returning them. If we keep the image of our part in this sphere (as Spirit), we can see that if we diminish our-Selves, we do not fill the space created for us. We are entitled to all of that room and we are obliged to keep that space filled. So, spread out, flex those Spiritual muscles and fill your space.

As we stay with this image of Spirit, we can leave the surface and become a part of the inside. Here, we are sub-*merged*, immersed. There is still a space for us, but we can imagine ourselves more like amoebae. We encounter many different beings, transfer feelings, move on and change. Our space is not so well defined on the inside, but it is still ours. The difference is that *within*, our own boundaries need not be so firm. They are more fluid and permeable. We can see ourselves as accepting, accessible, feeling beings without threat. All that we need is around us, all the time. All that we want is right here, right now. We are safe and at home – within Spirit. And, we are an essential part of All That Is.

It is such a comfortable, beautiful place to come to, that

it is difficult to leave. But, conscious earth-bound thoughts eventually return. You must rejoin this world. You will find if you do this exercise each morning, however, you can return to that place of tranquility without too much trouble during your day. The beauty and serenity you have *envisioned* are real. It is as easy as remembering. Remember the place where you grew up? Remember where you were when you experienced your first kiss? It's as easy as that. Just remember your part in "The Great Mind of God."

There is an old story about a man who was held captive in a cell. He had but one tiny window in the wall opposite the door, and he spent all of his hours, clutching the bars of that window, trying to see a speck of sunlight. He longed for the Light, but couldn't see very much of it through that tiny little window. Nevertheless, he kept looking, kept trying.

One day, he turned away from the window. He turned around and saw that the cell door was open!

I love this story. It reminds me that all I have to do is turn around. In my life, the window is "my will". The cell door is "Thy Will." Whenever my eyes get too strained from seeing from "my will", or my hands get calluses from hanging on (!) to the bars of "my will," I can turn around and see the door to something better, something unimaginable by me:

"Thy Will."

Freedom.

It occurred to me, one day, that as surely as the Universal Spirit, or my Higher Power, flows THROUGHOUT my Being, so does it flow OUT THROUGH my being. As long as I keep the "channel" clear, I can be an expression and illustration of Spirit. No effort is necessary, just letting go.

THE LORD'S PRAYER

The way I interpret The Lord's Prayer, the teacher, Jesus of Nazareth, was telling us that "This is the way it is. If you will see it this way, your life will be easier." Here is my interpretation of what he gave us in this simple prayer:

From the top: "Our Father, who art in heaven." Heaven, to me is the ideal – our highest thoughts. So, that which we are addressing in this prayer is the One who abides in our highest thoughts: the one who is in "heaven", Purity, Sanity, and Love, the highest concepts.

"Hallowed be thy name." Whatever name I choose to call this One is holy. I may choose "God", "Higher Power", Buddha", "Mother Nature", "The Universal Power", anything. But the name by which I call the ONE is sacred. That sets this ONE apart from the many, the common.

"Thy kingdom come, Thy will be done on earth as it is in heaven." Again, heaven is our highest thoughts. So, "Thy Kingdom", and "Thy Will" are to be made manifest in our daily lives ("on earth") as they are in our Highest Thoughts. The ideal world and our Highest Good can be real-ized in our earthly, daily, practical lives.

"Give us this day our daily bread." This is the promise. Everything we need is given to us each day. In Psalm 23, in the Old Testament, we are told "I shall not want." This is simply another way of stating the same Law. All we need is provided to us, every day. It is our choice to see it, to use it, to receive it, to accept it – whatever it is we are to do with it – we are offered it. Its availability is assured. Our acceptance of it is our option.

"And forgive us our debts as we forgive our debtors." Another Law of the Universe: As we release the resentments of the past, we are released. When we drop the weight of our own grudges, we are relieved. We are free.

"And lead us not into temptation, but deliver us from evil." This statement is particularly meaningful, I believe, to those of us in recovery from any obsession, compulsion or addiction. We are NOT left in, or lead into a state of unmanageability, "into temptation". When we follow The Law, and trust in The One, we give over the control we thought we had to The One who/which truly has it. We are DELIVERED from the less-than-good of our own making! The "evil" is our own judgments and our own mis-conceptions. We are not condemned to stay in our own "evil" – :

"For Thine is The Kingdom, and The Power": because The One has all things ('The Kingdom), and has all power. "And", finally, our own humility is necessary for it to work for us: "the Glory, Forever." Let us not take credit for the miracle of our lives. Give the "Glory" to the ONE.

"Amen."

INTO RECOVERY

THE FIRST THREE STEPS . . .

After some years in a 12-Step Program, some years of hearing the same things over and over in our meetings, and some years of some (?) sanity, some good (i.e. sanity-promoting) habits have begun to appear in my life. One such habit is to begin my day with the first three steps as outlined in the Big Book of Alcoholics Anonymous, the text upon which most 12-Step programs are based.

"1) We admitted we were powerless over alcohol, that our lives had become unmanageable." Once we admit that, we are saying, in effect, that alcohol (*or gambling, or over-eating, etc.) is a power greater than ourselves. Yep! Anything we are powerless OVER, is a power greater than ourselves. Right? Right. So, ALCOHOL* is the "bad power." If we were to stop at that step, we would be left in a pretty dismal condition. Unmanageability. But we are not, because Step 2 tells us that we:

"2) Came to believe that a Power greater than ourselves could restore us to sanity." So, we have found that there is ANOTHER power greater than ourselves; One that could restore us to sanity. "Good Power." Hope glimmers bright before us. We have a decision to make. To which power will we turn our day over? To which master will we pay homage? Well, then there's Step:

"3) Made a decision to turn our will and our lives over to the care of God as we understood him." That's our choice. For me, it is best for me to make this choice every morning, consciously. I like to assay my situation by reviewing the first step, then the second, and giving over to the third. There is such comfort I have found in "the care of God." That's the most obvious CHOICE to make, the most self-loving choice, the choice of HEALTH.

Once having made this 3rd Step decision, I get to make it several times during the day. For me, I don't do it enough, because I get caught up in my own "power", which I call my responsibilities, my duties, my abilities. Often in the course of my day, I sub-consciously try to "Give God the day off." I get turned around in my head, and think that I can handle situations all alone. Particularly predicaments. The longer I stay in recovery, though, the less time it takes for me to recognize that it is time to call in my Higher Power. That's progress.

If my day gets started without my taking the time to review these steps, I find the road has more speed bumps. It is then, that I can start my day over, to begin it again, by going through the Steps. It gets better!

THE ROAD TO SANITY

It occurred to me this morning that I was on the road to sanity. Just as quickly, it occurred to me that we all are! The road is our life and our journey. Unfortunately, we are all not moving in the same direction – in fact, some of us are not even moving.

I think that when we are born, this road is a very straight and smooth one. No variances, no bumps. Very quickly, however, obstacles appear in our way. We learn how to circumvent some of the spikes placed before us by parents, friends, life-situations. There are pits, too, and we do fall – most of us – into them. Some of us fall repeatedly. After several falls, some of us back away and assess the pits. Sometimes we are able to get past them. Then, we might fall into another one. Some of us, after falling numerous times, no longer even try to get out. Our attempts have been unsuccessful and the very idea of even trying to prevail appears futile. Few, if any of us, successfully circumvent every pit-fall.

In all of these travails, most of us start putting up our own roadblocks. It is survival, we think, and we do the best we can with the tools available to us. Time and time again, we try to gain different results from the same coping behavior. Without knowing it, WE have created a U-Turn. We are no longer headed toward sanity. The signs are distorted, reversed, and the road becomes a circle. We continue, but in what direction? When, at last, we are face-down in the pavement, we must ask for help. This is when we start our trudge anew.

As for myself, I realized that I had mis-perceived a lot. I always knew there was a Higher Power. Somewhere along my life, though, I began to think I wasn't spiritually tall enough to go on His Ride. I began to lose my-Self: my Self-esteem, my Self-regard and my Self-love. It all got lost in the opinions and actions of others. More powerfully, it got lost in MY mire of mis-understanding. I was falling into a pit, and it started to fill up with tar. I was stuck!

I felt as if I was filled with tar, instead of a whole self. In place of my soul, I saw lack, darkness and hopelessness. The downward spiral started, I obliterated the road signs and turned them over. My life had no luster, no appeal, no joy. It was like the black-and-white portion of the film "The Wizard of Oz." The louder I laughed, the more it hurt, and the more it hurt, the louder I laughed. The din was so loud that I could no longer hear "the still small voice". Tar was filling my ears, my eyes and my heart. I had no ambition to LIVE because I couldn't see LIFE as it was.

An advertising campaign tells us to get "the right tool for the job." There is more to it than that, but it is a good first step. Then, we have to make the effort and get into action.

In any kind of 12-Step and/or Spiritual self-help program, we are guided into the right direction and handed the right tools to build safe walk-ways over the pits. We are given compasses to tell us in what direction we are headed, and we are given the encouragement to MOVE.

In my experience, a dear friend who had held similar mis-conceptions showed me a ladder out of the pit. It had worked for him; maybe it could work for me. I now see that by choosing the task at hand, I can find LIFE and all of its joy, love and opportunities. Like the film, again, I have been able, now, to see my LIFE in COLOR!!! It takes a commitment to my-Self. I must remind myself each morning that I am worth the steps it takes to move TOWARD sanity. The old coping skills, which no longer serve me, are still lurking in my old tool box. It takes a conscious decision to sort through, assess the situations and select the "right tool for the job."

The road doesn't magically become safe and smooth again. It probably won't. But each of us can make the road passable at all times. We can choose to walk through the overgrowth, or cut it down. We can do what is necessary to get to the next clearing, the next oasis. And when we get there, we can laugh with those who have also reached that clearing. We can dance with those who have gone beyond, but are willing to reach back and help us through the next rough spot. We don't have to do it alone.

Fellowship is what I call this new toolbox. Therein lies the faith to get us to the next clearing. Therein lie the experience, strength and hope of those who have trudged the road before us. Therein lie the tools with which we can pave the way for those to come after us on – The Road to Sanity!

Most of the preceding essays were written when Mrs. Dries was Ms. Swarbrick. She was fortunate to get to know herself and appreciate herself enough to be fully ready to accept a single life. Not a life alone, but not a married life.

As a result of her self re-evaluations, her intro-inspections and her wonderful friends and guides, she became ready and willing to relate to new people in her life. The following is a true story, made possible, for her part, only by her willingness and readiness. She didn't *need* to meet a man. She wasn't *lacking* a part of her life or herself. She was happy and whole, when . . .

MY SIDE OF THE STORY

A dear friend of mine had a box full of video copies of feature films. He asked me to deliver them to the Actors' Fund for their housing unit devoted and designed for people with HIV. (You might think it odd that I am beginning my story by telling about the largess of a friend. Patience! It will make sense.) I agreed to this plan immediately, as I do volunteer work regularly in the same building where the Actors' Fund maintains an office.

After dropping off the tapes, I ran into another acquaintance of mine who works for the Actors' Fund. He was currently involved in planning a benefit concert and offered me two free tickets. One day earlier, I would have told him I was not available. One day earlier, I was scheduled to teach the first of a two-day master class in San Jose, but one day earlier it was canceled due to low enrollment. Two months earlier, I would have told him I was unavailable because I was going to a spiritual retreat with another great friend of mine. I had to cancel on the retreat because of the class. The cancellation of the class left me with a lot of unscheduled time.

A note here: I tend to fill my time, efficiently or productively or not – it is filled*.

So, I accepted his kind offer and began wondering whom I would invite to accompany me to the concert. I happened to check a monthly horoscope guide around this time and read that on the date of the concert, my "romantic life would experience a dramatic change." Now, I take these horoscope advisories with a grain of salt. But, I do read them. So, as I had been single for long enough in my lifetime, this particular item certainly persuaded me to think carefully about my extra ticket.

There was a writer/yoga teacher I had seen a few times, and I asked him, but he was too busy. Harumph! Then, I asked the fellow who had given me the tapes to donate to the Actors' Fund. Nope. He, too, was busy.

That evening, I was having dinner with two friends and one of them mentioned that his god-father was coming through town that weekend. He went on to describe his god-father as an adventurer (he had been to Nepal the previous year and would be returning soon to do more trekking and volunteer teaching). He took retirement from teaching the year previous, and toured the country on a part-time job in which he escorted groups of sports fans to major league baseball games. There was an exuberance in my friend's description of this man which encouraged me to ask the unspeakable: "Do you suppose he'd like to go this concert with me?" A blind date???? I was *asking* to have a blind date? Good grief. What was I, a masochist? Everyone knows how blind dates go. They are painfully boring, and excruciatingly long, no matter how brief. Nevertheless, I asked the question. My friend said, "Well, I don't know. I'll ask him."

That evening, after dinner, he e-mailed his god-father and it was done. There was no retrieving the invitation. It had been made and sent. So, then, I had to wait to see if this was going to happen, or if I was going to do what I normally did when I was offered two tickets to anything and that is to invite my very best friend who happens to be gay.

I want to make it clear here, that I adore my best friend. There is simply no way, however, to experience a "dramatic change in my romantic life" when I am with him. We are as thick as thieves, we have no secrets and we tend to hang so closely together that no one can get between us. I didn't want to live my life according to my horoscope, but neither did I want to bar the door against any chance that it could be accurate! So, I waited.

Two days later, the day before the concert, the god-father had communicated his willingness to go to the concert with me to his god-son. I didn't know whether to be relieved or panicked. I chose both. Now, I had to decide on wardrobe, when I should pick him up; there were lots of details that filled my time.* I was contented – along with relieved and panicked.

I arrived at my friends' house about 5 minutes early. My blind date came out into the living room, and immediately greeted me with a kiss on the cheek. He was not as tall as they had said, but not at all a disappointment. Here was a very distinguished-looking gentleman in his 50's, a little taller than I, (had I worn the wrong shoes????) seemingly very secure in himself. "Oh, no," I thought. "He's confident. He'll never NEED me." He was very attractive and appealing in that self-assured, crazy-making way. We sat for a few minutes, at my suggestion, and I explained that I would have to know his last name because I would be introducing him to some people at the event. Jim Dries, pronounced "Dreese".

There, that was done. We decided to leave, and with humorous instructions from his god-son to have him home by midnight (!) we were off. As soon as we left the house and were headed for my car (a sassy Mustang convertible – with the top down) I jokingly apologized to Jim Dries for not getting him a wrist corsage for the evening. Since I was picking him up and driving, I explained, that really was my responsibility. He, also jokingly, agreed and told me that as a result of my negligence, his feelings were hurt. The evening was thus set. I knew we would have a good time. His sense of humor was a perfect complement to mine. (Uh-oh!)

As we drove to the site of the concert, a huge Beverly Hills Estate, we talked. We didn't interview each other, as is so often the case. We were honestly interested in each other. I couldn't believe this man was really interested in what I had done. He was the one, it seemed to me, who had lived the exciting life. In addition to being a social studies teacher in New York State, he had lived in Hawaii and the Philippines. He had first been to Nepal in the Peace Corps. He was brought up in Iowa as a Catholic and had even studied for a few years in the seminary. Although he decided to leave the Catholic Church, he did not reject all the traditions and the rituals that had given him comfort. He was on a Spiritual quest not unlike my own. This was one incredible person. And, in great physical shape. For heaven's sake, he was trekking in the Himalayas!

There was never a moment of discomfort or unease with us. We were genuinely interested and authentically enjoying each other and the evening.

We arrived at the estate. Jacketed young men took my car for valet parking and we entered the street – level of the house. I introduced him to a couple of people and we were directed out to the "backyard." There we found several levels of activities, the lowest of which was the tennis court-cum-concert theatre. At the first level, there was an open bar. He asked me what I'd like and I told him a diet soda. I had already told him in the car that I was a recovering alcoholic, but I reassured him that it wouldn't bother me at all if he had a cocktail. He explained to me that he has the occasional beer or cocktail when it felt appropriate, but it felt appropriate on that evening for him to have a glass of juice. (What a guy!)

Shortly thereafter, a youngish gentleman came and introduced himself to me. He had worked at the office where I do volunteer work some years before. He recognized me from there and struck up a conversation. Soon afterwards, his partner joined us. We were talking about their recent adoption of a baby. Some friends of mine then appeared and I was talking with them. Occasionally, I would turn to Jim, who was deep in conversation with the two men. It was funny because we actually turned to each other simultaneously, just to see if the other was okay. I felt a little guilty that I had left him to fend for himself in this (what I thought was) totally alien-to-him world. He was fine. Once, when he left to go to the rest room, he met a man in line for the men's room. That man had written a book about a pact he and his lover had made before the lover's passing away. They were both HIV+, and promised each other that whichever one died first, that one would send signals back to the surviving lover. The author had an extra copy of his book with him, and after talking to Jim in line for a bit, determined that the reason he had brought the extra copy, and that they were waiting in line together, was that Jim should receive the book. Extraordinary! I am impressed with anyone who can hold a conversation with a mere acquaintance. This Dries fellow was making friends of total strangers. He was at ease with himself and everyone about him. And, he put me at ease. I didn't realize until later on how threatening his confidence could be to my partner-less status!

At last we were told to move down to the concert area. Jim offered his arm to me as we descended the steps. I accepted and felt like quite the lady – with quite a gentleman.

We both enjoyed the concert, which ended with a sing-along. "Our Love Is Here To Stay". How prophetic – though I certainly had no hint of that at the time. I still couldn't believe this man would find anything about me intriguing. I did, however, notice that he was looking at me as much as the chanteuse during the sing-along. Luckily, it was in good key for me, too. There were a few chits-and-chats with others after the concert, but we left soon after its conclusion. While we were waiting for the jacketed young men to get my car we spoke about this fabulous home in which we had enjoyed the evening. He had told me that following his divorce, about two years prior, he had put everything in storage except that with which he traveled. I joked about his trying to fit all the furniture from his "estate" into storage. He countered with a very serious telling about how the most difficult thing about it was saying good-bye to his garden-staff. Again, I felt so comfortable with this man. He was so much fun and sincerely interested in EVERYTHING.

As I drove us to his god-son's house, he asked if I wanted to stop for dessert or something. I said I was fine, but asked if he wanted to stop. He replied that he was fine, too, but that he didn't want the evening to end. Neither did I! We found an open coffee shop, and talked some more.

He told me he was leaving the next morning for the Bay Area. He would escort a group of those sports fans to a couple of baseball games there. In addition, he would see his son and his partner, and help his elder daughter and son-in-law with their newly growing family. They had recently had their third son and Jim was spending a good deal of time helping through the summer. A week later I was due to drive up to Sacramento, about an hour-and-a-half from the Bay Area, to begin a three-week engagement playing "Dolly Levi" in HELLO, DOLLY! We talked about meditation, we talked about sports, we talked about everything. I was so charmed and fascinated by him. I really wanted to talk more, to see him again, but I had already realized how impractical and improbable that would be.

We finally left the coffee shop and found our way to the house. We were there at 11:30 – clearly before the aforementioned curfew. I didn't park the car because I didn't know how to proceed, now that we were back. We said a few clumsy "Good-bye's", and he suggested that we might be able to get together up north when we were both there. ("Oh, sure," I thought. "Out of sight, out of mind!" I thought.) A few more "Well, see ya."

Then, he kissed me. Wow! And, I kissed him back. Well, we kissed and kissed. At last, he suggested I put the car in "Park" and turn off the headlights. I did, and we kissed some more. It was like we were teenagers. We fogged up the windows, and we were just kissing. It was so sweet and innocent – and it seemed to be impossible for us to say

"Goodbye". About two hours later, he did get out of the car, and, promising to call me again, went to the house. I drove away praying that he *would* call me and that we would see each other again.

The next day, I had a morning appointment but came back home for a few minutes in the early afternoon. Just as I was leaving my townhouse, there was an elderly delivery man with a vase full of red roses coming down the walkway. I saw them and wished they were for me. I love flowers, especially when they are sent to me. He said "These flowers are for Unit #14." (I live in Unit #4) I explained to him that the building only goes up to Unit #9. ("Could it be a little error in the address?" I wondered. "Could they possibly be for me????" I hoped.) He said, "Well these are for a Carol Swarbrick."

"That's me! They're for me!" I nearly yelled at this frail man. He just grinned and handed them to me, saying, "Well, that was good timing, wasn't it?". I took them inside, sat down, read the card and cried. Jim had sent me red roses, with a note that read "The reviews are unanimous. You are sensational. Hope to see you soon."

* * *

That was the beginning. On August 3, 2001, Jim Dries and Carol Swarbrick were married – and the saga continues. Read the whole story in their forthcoming book: *A 21st Century Love Story, A Romance for All Ages.*

The following page is to be clipped out, your name inserted where indicated and placed in a frequently seen location. Frame it, mount it, hang it, whatever you want. But remember, it is true about YOU!

CERTIFICATE OF SUFFICIENCY

It is understood and appreciated that the person named herewith has been found to be Whole and Complete.
It is also recognized and agreed, that this same person is
Plenty.
Therefore, by the very fact that we are all created out of, by and from
The Allness,
Right Now and Forevermore,

(your name)
Is hereby acknowledged to be
ENOUGH